# The Wheels of Life: (dis)Ability Poetry Collection

Cassie Liviero

The Wheels of Life: (dis)Ability Poetry
Collection © 2023 Cassie Liviero

All rights reserved.

No part of this publication may be
reproduced, stored in a retrieval system, or
transmitted, in any form or by any means,
electronic, mechanical, photocopying,
recording, or otherwise, without the prior
written permission of the presenters.

Cassie Liviero asserts the moral right to be
identified as the author of this work.

Presentation by *BookLeaf Publishing*

Web: www.bookleafpub.com

E-mail: info@bookleafpub.com

ISBN: 9789357613194

First edition 2023

# DEDICATION

This is dedicated to my family, friends and helping professionals whom I appreciate so much.

You all hold different significances in my life, but each one of you helped shape this collection.

You are my community.

This collection combines truth, humour, love, hope and inclusion. My lived experiences as a wheelchair user have shaped this collection. I hope to create awareness and spaces for change.

# ACKNOWLEDGEMENT

To (dis)Abled communities. Times are not up yet, live interconnected. To a society stuck in transition, thanks for the lessons.

# PREFACE

This is a space for (dis)Abled poetry only. Due to lack of funding all mainstream programs have been suspended, turning our attention to those with (dis)Abilities. If you are not (dis)Abled and are interested in participating, please put your name on the waitlist, and our selection committee will be in touch to set up an interview.

Censorship of ableist comments or experiences is strictly prohibited.

This collection intends to get audiences to think and question some potential assumptions and what some might take for granted. Additionally, I invite readers to reflect on what is working, and for potential allies to give a voice to underrepresented populations to continue their interpretations and continue their writing.

I don't think that I know everyone's (dis)Ability experiences. When I refer to 'I' it is because I'm speaking from my personal experience, from the heart.

The use of the word 'YOU 'does not suggest personal responsibility, but references wider society.

In my opinion, this poetry continues to be
unfinished. No matter how many readers pick up
this book, no single experience is the same.
This is just the beginning of a long journey.

Email: Thewheelsoflife@gmail.com

# The Wheels of Life

My wheels of life have been a study companion
They have been with me and impacted me since the
beginning of their time
But they're not all of me. They celebrated with me
Sat silently with me, in motion without the use of my
legs
they challenge me,
they show me innovation
at times there is heartache.
The wheels run me over
I hope the wheels keep turning as we recreate an
authentic future with creativity, innovation and
difference
The wheels will be able to carry and circle other
communities
they are the perfect shape for creating continuance
May people be able to use the cogs of their wheels to
create a position in which they feel they fit perfectly
Hopefully, there are other communities of wheels that
will roll in solidarity
I'm not pretending that this will be easy, accepted or
supported.
Wheels and communities in motion fit better when
they travel together

# Ableism Is

Ableism is assuming resistance is ungratefulness or stubbornness
Ableism is being inspired by our existence
Ableism is thinking you know best
Ableism is believing that accommodations mean less work
Ableism is assuming we want and need to be fixed
Ableism is reducing our lives to dollar signs
Ableism is a lack of opportunity or resources
Ableism is assuming strength and time heal you
Ableism is a lack of responsibility
Ableism is silencing voices
Ableism is underpaid work because of (dis)Ability
Ableism is checkboxes proof and application forms
Ableism is survival
Ableism is prioritizing what essential needs matter
Ableism is endless self-marketing and promoting
Ableism is shaming bodies and abilities
Ableism is limiting possibilities by minimizing (dis)Ability as a change agent
Ableism starts and ends with YOU

SAME STRUGGLE
DIFFERENT DIFFERENCE
I HAVE A DREAM

# I am

I am more than my (dis)Ability, but still, need your help
I am powerful when heard
I am strong but not indestructible
I am patient but not aimless
I am shifting but not disappearing
I am accountable but not sorry
I am loving but won't be unlovable
I am learning but knowledgeable
I am open to your words, but I'll tell you how I feel
I can forgive but expect change
I am seen but not special
I am okay being alone but will resist isolation
I am (dis)Abled, but together we are able

# Stare

Stare, but don't be afraid
Stare, but know we're headed in the same direction
Stare, but know we all have 24 hours in a day; mine
were productive too-
Stare, but know I'm a woman
Stare, but realize my wheelchair is a vehicle just like
your car
Stare, but know I see you
Stare, but know my fork doesn't talk or the food I eat
with it
Don't stare or ask others - speak to me. I bet I'll
surprise you with my answers

# The Wheelchair Genie

With the flick of my wrist, I push my chair forward
I lean it back like I'm laying on clouds
I can make knowledge read and write
Make connections beyond the width of the stage
I can communicate all day and night
The crowd goes wild as imaginary
'try me' buttons light up the room
Talking, moving, thinking too!
The stage is mine
I can fill it up with the flick of the wrist, tongue,
cheek, and jaw!
A young boy running toward me, happy
I twirl him using my chair
I get cards just for being there
People come up and touch my soft hands
I ponder my day and wonder when cash will be in the
hat
I wouldn't mind a few more knickknacks
I smile to myself, but I am tired
I will go home eat, sleep and stretch my brain to
maximum power.
If you thought today was inspirational
Next time can you throw me 100 or two?

# The Reveal

May there be less of a need to window shop
To learn through the process of elimination
To compare and analyze yourself
To choose the least harmful option
To sacrifice well-being
To figure it all out
To say you're okay
To work so hard
To never give in
To have endless energy
To keep searching
To build your future
To get it just right
There is only one of you
You must be valuable
You must be true
Suppose it looks like the truth is not possible
Then, believe it takes more than you

# Times Not Up

Times not up yet
Times not up yet. Hold on tight
Times are not up yet. Hold on tight
Blast that music
Talk it out.
Write
Create something only you can understand.
It's for nobody's eyes, ears, or heart but yours.
Hold On Tight.
Times are not up yet.
Don't settle for less. Speak out loud.
You know what you need
Repeat, repeat.
Advocate. just hold on tight
times not up yet
People don't know you as you know, you
Time is yours because times not up yet.
As long as you choose to be here, people and support
are responsible for giving you time.
As long as you're here, times not up yet because you
are accomplishing living

# Don't tell. Don't Scare

Don't tell. Don't scare
Don't tell, don't offend
Don't be meek, but self-monitor
Be productive but independent
Feel but don't cry
Be knowledgeable, not overbearing
Be powerful but know your place
Tell your story but don't write the chapters
Fight but don't win
Despite this, own your story write the chapters the
way you know and create them
Disrupt the status quo, be powerful
Your story may help someone else begin to rise and
thrive

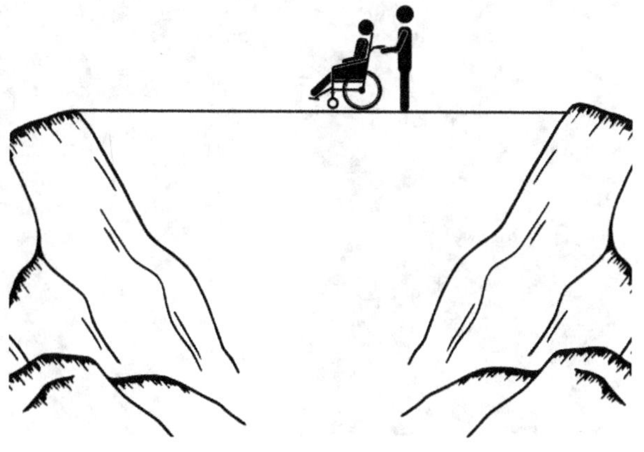

# I Know

I know your fears hold a passion
I know your loneliness holds a vision
I know your pain has a rich history
I know your authenticity is love
I know your anger is knowledge
I know your breakdowns are moments for connection
I know your need to structure is about necessity and independence
I know your words are opportunities to listen
I know your questions are opportunities to reflect
I know your situation allows me an opportunity to challenge myself and grow
I know your life is yours

# Love Loud

Love loud, and question
Love loud and be proud
Love loud and act
Love loud but change what love sounds like and should be
Love loud from the outside in
Love loud and integrate
Love loud and find a way
Love loud and say yes
Love loud and know that every bit matters
Love loud and feel the importance
Love loud and hold steady
Love loud and connect to your values
Love loud but like no one is watching
Love loud, and you will be able to feel the quiet and unique vibrance of those around you

# Diamond in the Rough

I am not a superhero, but I can move fast
I am not special but rather badass
I have learned to navigate this world in these
changing times
It is a prerequisite but I'm not gonna sign
Times are not changing for me, and my wheelchair
and even hocus pocus won't end the love we share
Often we're off balance because life is such a
challenge
But we can make it work when humour is mixed with
the hurt
Use your imagination, laughter, love, and play
You know your world and ways from the start
Speak out loud and from the heart

# The Humanity Principal

Heal in being heard
Utilize community. Uproot assumptions
Manifest your vision
Access = acceptance of your authentic self
Niche (Create a)
Independent and interconnected (Be)
Take Back your power
You are enough

# The Re-Awakening

Energy work is a flowing life force
Freedom from limitations.
Freedom from your mind.
Complete acceptance. Your body is working for you.
Every part of you is working with more and more
ease
Your body and mind are not against you.
Not talking, for, to or about you, except to show you
love.
The fight has quieted between your mind, body, and
soul
Things will release as needed. Give yourself
permission
Be in the moment.
Be with the flow of life.
(Dis)Ability will never change.
But it is possible.
You can get your body and mind to work for you with
proper support, not against you.
Your body can show you compassion and receive it.
It is possible to be at one with the world and not feel
guilty about it.
Our bodies and our minds can do right by us, and you
deserve the opportunity to experience this
Whatever it looks like for you. And whatever you
need in the process
This experience is all about you
Ask for expression, ask for support.

You're not any less worthy because you're not doing this alone. However long it takes.
You are safe and protected here. No masks, you are you and only you
You are doing it, and your body and mind are showing you a different way.
Let things unfold and grow to be mindful,
Let your body go, let your heart unfold, and let people meet your needs in the process.

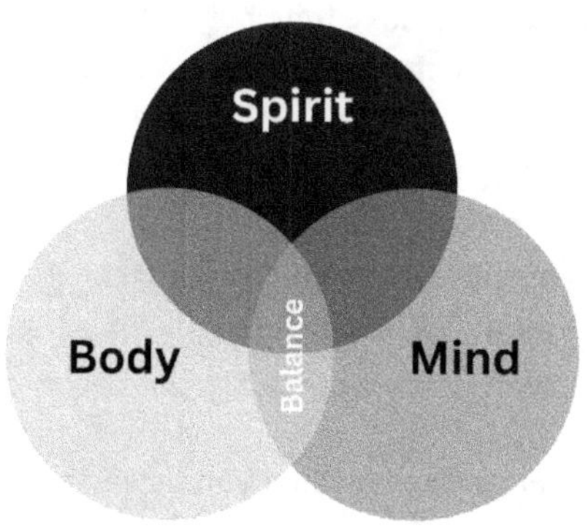

# The Treatment Room

I come in you think you know my story
Pen ready, you have me figured out
I am searching for the words that make sense things
that are real
I'm drowning in your clinical babble
You're inaccessible, just like the office
You're telling me to change my thoughts but remain
unaffected, by what I share
You tell me things take time but rush my process
You try and cure me with logic and assume my own
is faulty
You can have expectations, but mine are unattainable
Shadows are okay with light
Pain is okay but must be time-limited
Living is okay, but survival is dangerous

---

I know healing begins when you listen and learn my
story
When pens are down, and souls are invested
When you speak from a place of vulnerability rather
than a textbook
When you value time and your contribution to it
When you accept that logic comes from lived
experience and trust my words and actions
When you realize the expectations I have, place value
and commitment on myself, the relationship, and the
healing process

When you believe that through shadows and pain,
voices in their purest form are validated
When you know that survival is the deepest act of
self-respect and love
When you are humbled and honored to walk beside
me, not in front of me
When you hold my load with me
When you remember your pain
When we are human

# Natural Metamorphosis

The natural lifecycle of the tree as it drops its leaves
Predators become naturally instinctual when they feel
endangered.
Animals intuitively go back to different habitats as
they wait out the winter months.
Snakes that shed skin
Butterflies that cocoon until they are ready to
transform
Flowers that bloom.
Eggs that hatch
Babies that cry then learn to interact with the world
We are all capable of natural metamorphosis. Take
action. Don't wait.
Let's begin this process by putting marginalized
voices front and center
The rest will happen naturally
Like spiders spinning a web
We can step out of our web to gain a deeper
understanding and knowledge.

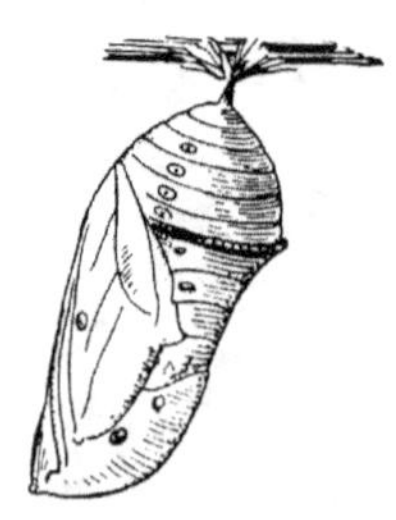

# A Game of Risk

Travel is not a choice; travel is not the act of getting
to and from places
It has little to do with raising fuel prices or owning a
vehicle
The traffic on the roads of life halting my
spontaneity.
I thump schoolbooks, not stadiums
I don't navigate shopping malls; I navigate my ability
to wear what is sold
I don't book travel agents; I recruit help for my next
bathroom trip or school assignments
Money is not access to travel; money is compensation
to travel to the shower to the subsequent
appointments if my agents will take on the risk
without knowing where they are landing
They may hit all the stop lights, and I will have to
navigate roundabouts
I take route after route to be able to access my home,
my life, my community
It's not a commuter's dream, but the journey is more
manageable with more passengers.

# The Power of Expression

I am continuously examining the power of words.
The way they are used have the power to divide and
unite people.
As human beings, we have an incredible gift to be
able to create language.
Language, that can be heard and received by others.
We can accomplish this by beginning to unlearn what
we have seen and been taught about (dis)Ability
So, I ask you how are you using your ability to
mobilize language?
Have you thought about the power you've been given
to share, receive or resist the language of others as
humans communicate the meanings of their lives
Persons with (dis)Abilities often are placed in
positions where they must interact with systems that
make the language of change impermeable
Sometimes diagnosis doesn't even place someone a
cut above the rest for support
How do we convey the views and needs of others
when they cannot use language, what is our
responsibility?
We must continue to use language to begin to initiate
so many shifts that are needed in the world.
Observe, but speak your truth.
Research, but share
Use language carefully and with intention
Stand up and know when it's time to sit

Society must push for the things that cannot be seen
or they won't come into view
Must push for the things that do not seem like viable
possibilities, or they will never become choices.
We must use language for a better tomorrow or to
make a small change today
Think, speak, share, and act

# Seize Your Day

The start of my day begins.
The personal support worker places the equipment to
lift me up and roll me from side to side. Then, putting
the sling under me.
It takes some time
My legs hold captive the pillow that was holding my
feet apart last night.
Tell my body to relax. Nope.
Move my legs. Wrong again
Sometimes it's a matter of performing a Houdini
move so we can quickly flip the pillow out from
underneath me.
Then there is the upper body torso.
I never knew my body was so good at the bulldozer
impression.
My morning routine is a lot like the bulldozer.
My sling is a padded scoop holding my body in a
cocoon-like shape, attached to a machine driven by
others to transport it. the goal is no body spillage
A backward maneuver to enter the bathroom as I am
on the commode chair
Back in my room for washing and powdering.
Attempt to get dressed.
I feel like the dressing process it's like a game of
operation. Touching my muscles before the stiff
'buzz' sounds the alarm
If my muscles react the wrong way, the buzzer takes
all!

Muscles one, clothes zero
My personal bulldozer and its gadgets ban together
once again back to my wheelchair
My hair is an easier beast to tame.
As I eat, I think to myself, there's not one way, there
is no right way, but there is our way

# Graduate EdYOUcation

Cripping education
One task at a time
Changing the meaning of the 'good' (dis)Abled
graduate student
Putting my voice forward to lessen the power of
other's voices
By redefining and expanding productivity
Knowing I am an expert in my own life
Questioning preference over necessities
By using creativity to open doors to possibility
Life experience is a vulnerable form of highly praised
critical analysis skills
To take up the space, I deserve

# Mix and Match

Mistrust, I am in the process of unlearning
Inflexible, I know what is right for me
Emotional, I am intuitive
Needy, I am interdependent
Overbearing, I am holding myself and others
accountable
Anxiety, I want to express your value
Lack of self-worth, I can be selectively authentic. I
can choose when to praise myself because I know my
self-worth and when others value it
Over analyzing, I have profound awareness and value
when others respect my need to prepare
Holds on to pain, I know what conditions allow me to
release. I will wait for them
Negative, my truth has value, I am realistic

# Finding Home

All too often my inner world feels disjointed and
restricted
I ask myself "where do I fit in this world?"
I look around and see mechanical lifts, assistive
devices, and a defective body
My answer: not with the 'normals'.
Inclusion criteria, the efficient performance of the
white able body.
When the "normals" come into contact with this
extraterrestrial community, the list of minimum
requirements will become a mission to abolish any
social emotional or physical differences
Thoughts and feelings squeeze my insides it's a
struggle to control my burning eyes
The expanding lump in my throat and my stiff
tingling body feel soulless, a human shell
My words are caught; the shadowy figures get louder
each carrying their own stories:
BROKEN
EXPECTATIONS
DEMORALIZED
INVISIBILITY
As my parents or support workers drop my daily
meds in my mouth they travel a short journey,
priming my preferred demeanor each pill taking on
my inner world
My shadowy figures rising dislodged from their
home within me

Each one takes its place, despite being in a seated
position in my wheelchair
My limbs are rigid due to muscle spasms my
phantom-like figures curl around my misshapen body
that could have and should have been 'normal'.
Surgeries didn't fix me, my phantom figures act like
an overly amused sideshow, still holding to hope that
anything can change if 'I put my mind to it'.
My feelings can drown me, and my inner world
leaves me to battle some of the harshest storms
These storms remain docile to onlookers 'the thriving
student, the genuine connector'.
I have an inner drive to live, see and create change.
This I am thankful and excited about, I am also hurt,
angry and exhausted.
My body is more than a site of inspiration, it carries
and has carried relentless emotional and physical pain
and is a site of endurance
My eyes carry a unified vision of humanity, while
they cry tears and watch fear grow.
My tongue has been silenced; my words have been
squelched
My words speak the language of solidarity to all
those with lifelong impairments.
(Dis)Abled communities don't have to accept a
society that (dis)Ables with words representations
lack of and sterile interactions
To my family I love you, I am forever grateful for
your endless support, thanks for all you give
physically and emotionally because of this, my life
extends far beyond my wheelchair

I so appreciate you're unwavering values of love,
inclusivity, adapting and spontaneity
To my friends, thank you for your deep love and
commitment
You have taught me so much about strength and how
to be a radical and an authentic 'badass', love you all.
To my professors and mentors, your teaching has
enabled me to write and connect to my own voice.
To redefine and recreate a world based on social
justice, self-acceptance, beauty, and autonomy.
So, this is a call to humanity are you willing to
sacrifice comfort?
Challenge yourself at a core level
This is not an individual responsibility
What role will you play?

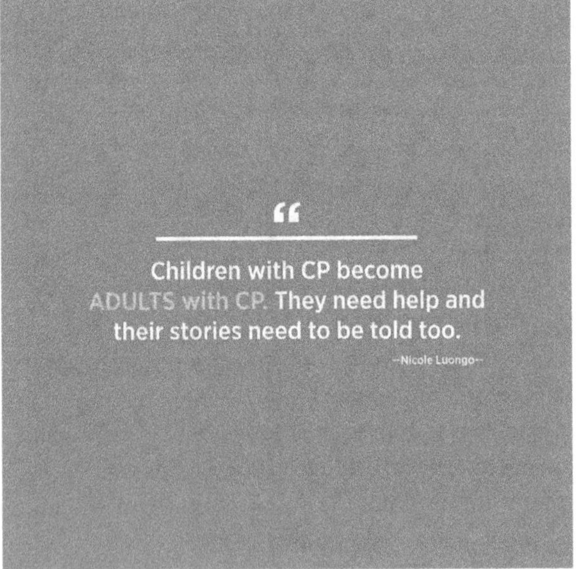